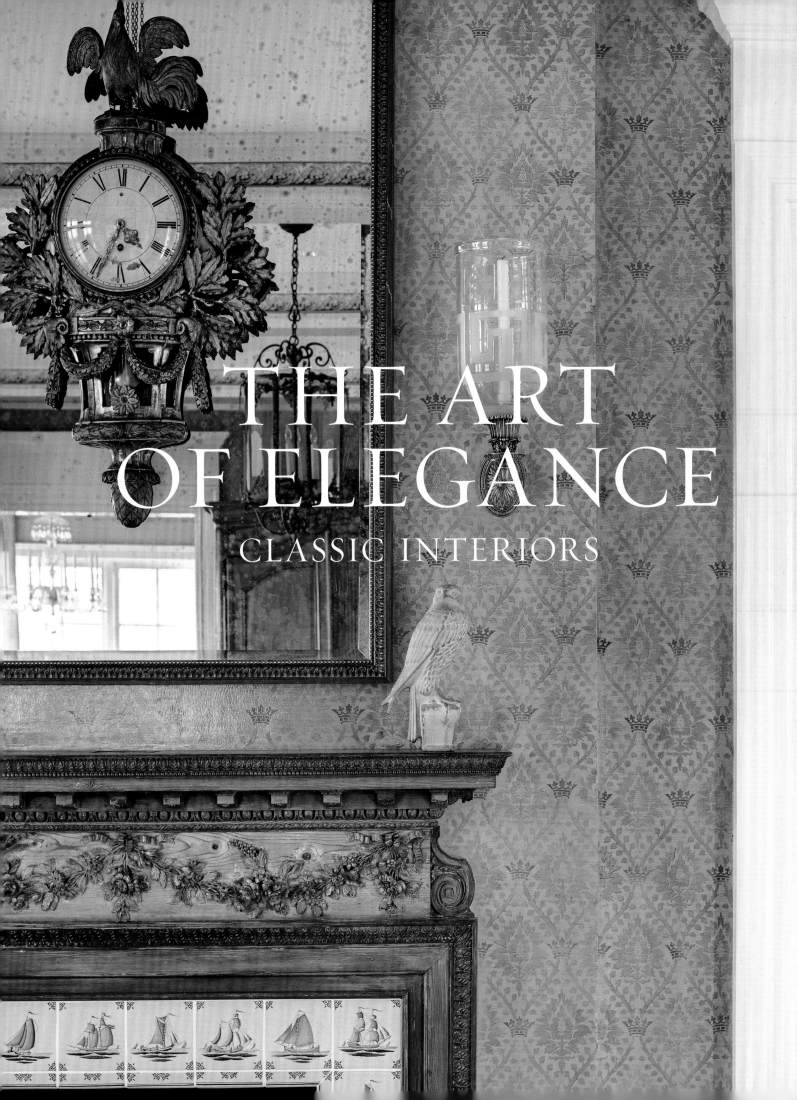

THE ART OF ELEGANCE

CLASSIC INTERIORS

THE ART
OF ELEGANCE

CLASSIC INTERIORS

MARSHALL WATSON

WRITTEN WITH MARC KRISTAL

RIZZOLI
NEW YORK

New York Paris London Milan

TO PAUL

AND

TO LILLY

CONTENTS

INTRODUCTION

have practiced the art and craft of interior design for nearly thirty years. And having been asked, on multiple occasions, what gives my firm its particular distinction, I've developed a succinct explanation: I use my talents, training, and experience—really, everything I've learned in the course of a lifetime—to become a conduit for other people's aspirations. The great playwright Samuel Beckett spoke of learning to write "without language." You might say that I have sought to design without a personal signature style: to absent myself to the greatest possible extent and make each project about realizing, and refining, my clients' most heartfelt fantasies of home.

As you will see, no two of my designs are alike. Nonetheless, I hope you will discover a consistency of vision and an approach to practice as distinct and indelible as a set of fingerprints, always underscored by a sense of elegance.

While I have consistently been someone with artistic impulses, they went in a variety of directions before I arrived at interior design (to the great chagrin of my mother, who advised me to "Focus on one thing, and do it well!"). Yet throughout my various careers, there has remained a continuity; no matter the field, I was always doing the same work.

I studied design at Stanford University, along with engineering and literature, and took each extremely seriously. My first aspiration was to be a fine art painter. I tried; but what I discovered was that I couldn't live that way. It wasn't me to be alone in a studio. More to the point, I didn't want what I did to be specifically about myself and my own vision, but instead more embracing—open to other people's ideas and aspirations. As an artist, I needed to interpret.

Given this recognition, and the fact that I was a well-schooled designer and an experienced painter, it proved a natural segue for me to move into theatrical design. I had the ability, I found, to analyze a text and interpret it into a stage set, and the challenge (and the fun) was that you went in an entirely different direction with each new production—we'd do a Neil Simon comedy one week, Shakespeare the next, and follow it up with an opera. For each, I would plunge into intensive research, a process I thoroughly enjoy, and that became

among my most essential creative tools. I was vitalized by the scenographer's core task: working with the director to crystallize the theme of a given script and develop a setting that supported and encouraged it—without calling excessive attention to itself. This proved to be excellent training for my present profession. In interior design, the "script" is the wishes of the clients, and I use my talents to create a home that supports and encourages a specific domestic narrative.

No less important to what I do today was the career that followed theater design: acting. If the former taught me how to transform the big idea of the play into a visual environment, the latter showed me the way to invest that drama with soul. My ambition was to be a character actor, someone who erases himself and is unrecognizable from role to role, a skill I pursued passionately. As with scenic design, I would do copious amounts of research and delve deeply into the mind, soul, society, and behavior of a particular role. Acting taught me so many skills of value to interior design: to ask my imagination a hundred questions; to be specific and honest in interpretation and expression; to remain receptive to the point of vulnerability; not to be stingy with myself; to submit my talents to the dreams and aspirations of my clients' "script"; to be committed to absolute quality in execution.

Perhaps most of all, both careers taught me, once I'd prepared, prepared, prepared, to throw it all away and trust my creativity. Chopin famously observed that "after one has played a vast quantity of notes and more notes, it is simplicity that emerges as the crowning reward of art." For me, that simplicity emerged from trusting that all the preparation I'd done would be there, and so it is in interior work as well.

In the end, as much as I loved the theater, my truest calling was design. It has been the work of three decades—half a lifetime—and there have been so many lessons. Unlike stage sets, homes are for people to live in and be comfortable, not for me to put my work or cleverness on display. I learned to craft interiors that supported the story of my clients' lives in a way that was domestic and intimate, rather than outward-looking and representational. Another, related lesson was not to privilege the object over the experience. At every scale, it can be tempting to show off. However, while I do believe there can be a star in a room, the supporting players and chorus are equally important—what genuinely matters is the overall gestalt. If all the energy in a space is wrapped around an heirloom armoire or a precious antique chair, chances are that the entirety won't flow together. Authentic success lies in serving the story—that is, the story of home.

Thus my projects may not scream "look at me," and you may ask, if my objective is to disappear into every role, then what makes a "Marshall Watson interior"—what constitutes my indelible set of fingerprints? My answer would be that, in all ways, I embrace the principles that transform a series of rooms into the true definition of elegance: Warmth. Light. Peace. Balance. Proportion. Livability. I aspire to create homes that are uplifting as well as comfortable, graceful as well as high-functioning, coherent as well as appropriate. This is my pursuit of the art of elegance.

It's said that our time on earth goes in cycles, that every seven years, you shed your life along with your skin. Perhaps that was true in my theatrical days. But my three-decade-long love affair with interior design shows no sign of abating. I come from a Kansas City family in which the enduring values—generosity above all— were honored and obeyed. One of them was humility, and in that spirit, I am grateful every day to be able to do what I do, to have found a place for my restless creative DNA to settle and flourish.

"Focus on one thing, and do it well," said my mother. It took a while, but I achieved the former. As for the latter—you be the judge.

FIFTH AVENUE CLASSIC

Permit me, for a moment, to brag about the home team: I always say that if you hire a New York interior designer, you're getting the best—because so many obstacles are thrown in our path that there's nothing we can't overcome, and the amount of finesse that's required to finish a space has no equal. Regarding the former, the average New York City apartment is like an archeological site, with the truth of a structure buried beneath so many layers of renovations, systems, and provisional fixes that you often have to demolish everything down to the studs to know what you're really dealing with. As for the latter, the simple fact is that because Gotham residences are so restricted spatially, you notice every finish, every detail—which means that everything a designer does needs to be perfect.

This residence, when I first saw it, exemplified these conditions. On the plus side, it was in a dream location: directly across Fifth Avenue from the majestic Beaux Arts façade of the Metropolitan Museum of Art, with views into the galleries containing the Met's incomparable collection of classical antiquities. Within, however, I found a classic prewar apartment—with classic challenges. The primary one had to do with scale: my clients' residence had originally been much larger, but at some point it had been subdivided, resulting in a situation in which the head—the entry hall and double parlor—was palatial, while the body was comprised of mostly undersized spaces that couldn't support the weight of that first impression. The place suffered from light issues as well: while the rooms overlooking Fifth Avenue received unobstructed western sun, in back there were only small windows opening onto a pair of inner courts. And apart from the beautiful walnut parquet floors, which we took pains to preserve, the interiors were in an advanced state of dilapidation.

And yet my clients had purchased on Manhattan's Upper East Side to enjoy a timeless New York living experience, in a building of undeniable pedigree, on an incomparable boulevard. So we set about seducing the place into becoming the stylish, livable residence it could be. No surprise: our major inspiration lay just across the street. My clients loved the Met's neoclassical style, shot through with a sense of the modern—and since the apartment looked directly into the museum's Greek and Roman galleries, we decided that the residence would be a de facto extension of them. Our goal was to craft a connection between New York's great public temple of the arts and the private domain in its shadow.

PREVIOUS PAGES: The foyer sets in motion three of this New York apartment's principal motifs: reflectivity, classicism, and the presence of dynamic art; Hellenic vases flank a contemporary statue in basalt—an artist's revisiting of the *Winged Victory of Samothrace*. The compelling presence of the French Deco and Austrian Biedermeier pieces in the foyer (which connects to the dining room, with its walls upholstered in Venetian silk velvet) sets the stage for the refined, striking glamour that is to come. At the northern end of the living room, a pair of Robert Adam-style mirrors, above shagreen consoles designed by my studio, flank a work by Alexander Calder; the Carrara marble mantelpiece is original to the residence. RIGHT: At the living room's southern end, a portal—flanked by Biederman and Bleckner paintings—leads to a newly created library; it frames the view of a colorful modern painting that remains entirely at home in its classic surroundings.

Working with the couple's architect, we reapportioned the square footage of the oversized original rooms, giving part of the entry hall to a new powder room, and sculpting a stately prelude to the master suite, a zone defined by a column screen in the style of Robert Adam. A third of the double parlor became a library, and we created axial connections between all the new spaces, to preserve intercommunication. Natural light, too, received thoughtful consideration: the parlor, library, and bedroom all overlook Fifth Avenue, while the formal dining room— which is used only at night, and benefits from controlled romantic illumination—is set on the inner court.

The plan reshaped, I gave the rooms a "modern neoclassical" treatment. The historic language is recognizable in the column screen and dentil moldings, and the baseboards and casings are slightly larger, simpler, more rectilinear. To differentiate the space from its immediate neighbor, we finished the library in walnut stained a rich plum-pudding mahogany, and gave it numerous coats of lacquer and a hand-buffed French polish. (Additionally, we crafted doors that fold away when opened, to become a continuation of the paneling.) Though

ABOVE: A carefully composed vignette in the foyer sparkles with mercury crystal, bronze doré, and richly polished burled chestnut. OPPOSITE: The library is paneled in French-polished zebra walnut and anchored by a magnificent silk Tabriz rug. The colorful sofa pillows were added after the Elizabeth Murray painting was installed, to more firmly connect the artwork to its setting, as do the electric blue mohair ottomans.

The bronze doré credenza serves as a formidable platform for the ephemeral sheaths of colored rice paper that make up the Hashimoto sculpture. The slightly overscaled casing that surrounds the portal connecting the living and dining rooms subtly draws the classical architecture into the modern age. My office designed the dining table, constructed from rare flitches of nineteenth-century Austrian burl, and the neoclassical rosewood chairs.

most of what existed was replaced, we retained the original nineteenth-century white marble mantelpiece in the living room, a reminder of Fifth Avenue style in its golden age.

Perhaps the greatest challenge involved making even the depths of the apartment shimmer with light, an effect achieved by selecting reflective materials. We invested much effort in finding the right stone for the graphic black-and-white floor of the entry, ultimately milling twenty-four-inch squares of a specific slab marble that conveys softness and transparency as well as high-key glamour. In the same space, rather than use conventional mirrors on the doors to the master suite, we collaborated with a stained-glass atelier to develop an antiqued poured mirroring that enriches the apartment's historic character. The living room walls, too, radiate illumination, from a gloss paint that references the color of the museum's limestone.

We chose to slightly underfurnish the rooms, to emphasize the strong silhouettes of the antiques and custom-designed pieces, as well as to give the apartment a sense of air. The polished wood, stone, and metal elements capture and reflect light, and the shimmer extends to the dining room's silk carpets and upholstered walls, which also dampen sound from the avenue below. The curtains, which were uplit, echo the dramatic monument lighting of the Met's façade across the street.

I was gratified to see that the couple's very contemporary art collection sat naturally and comfortably within a classical setting. In fact, an exquisitely executed classical envelope can accommodate a range of styles—because the simplicity, restraint, and purity of classical architecture exemplify what we prize about modernity. Rather than being at odds with one another, art, architecture, and décor are all mutually enriching.

In the kitchen/informal dining room, the marble-topped table, upholstered chairs, and weathered limestone floor add a note of informality while the refined nickel chandelier ties the space to the rest of the apartment.

Though it looks directly across Fifth Avenue (a mere three floors below) into the arched windows of the classical galleries of the Metropolitan Museum, the master bedroom remains an oasis of tailored serenity. My studio designed the upholstered headboard, flanked by mirrored nightstands. An elegant writing desk by Jules Leleu sits between the windows.

A REFINED REVIVAL

This classic California Mediterranean residence dates from the 1930s and has all the hallmarks of the genre: harmonious, well-proportioned volumes with Mission and Islamic references, a pantile roof, windows with distinctive parabolic arches. The house commands a prominent site as well, in a leafy old residential district with sycamore and oak trees below, aspens farther up the mountain, and sweeping views of downtown, the world-famous lake, and one of America's most spectacular capitol buildings.

If you have sensed a disconnect between my first and second sentences, you are correct: the place may be Mediterranean Revival in style, but it is located in Salt Lake City, not Los Angeles. And yet that's not as odd as it may seem—at least not to me: the street on which I grew up, in a handsome suburb, might have been characterized as an architectural petting zoo. Our house was French Norman. The one next door was Tudor. A Swiss chalet sat directly across the street, with a brick Southern Colonial beside it, opposite a Provençal château. While this might have induced a case of aesthetic *mal de mer* in a European, it was in fact the *haute* suburban norm in the years before the war. The houses may have been different, but a consistency of excellence served as the common denominator. And rather than suggesting a lack of sophistication, that embrace of variety captured an almost poignantly innocent, entirely American exuberance.

So I appreciated this Salt Lake City residence the moment I saw it, in a way a strict modernist might not—and in all fairness, it was hard to do so. The previous owner, a dentist with an apparently unquenchable passion for marble, had completely clad the interior in great green squares of the stuff, transforming it into a Marble-eum. There was also an extravagance of highly theatrical faux painting, which brought to mind a themed Greek restaurant; and, contributing to the antic air, a wing had been added to enclose a movie theater—a miniature version of a 1920s Asian-themed cinema palace, like Grauman's Chinese. Though highly imaginative, the treatments disguised the essence of the house.

PREVIOUS PAGES: I worked with the great landscape architect Garr Campbell on this historic Salt Lake City residence. Garr's Islamic-influenced limestone and marble fountains meshed elegantly with the North African origins of the home's Mediterranean Revival style. LEFT AND OPPOSITE: Taking advantage of a superb local decorative ironwork studio, I adapted a motif I'd seen in a historic house south of San Francisco for the design of the gates separating the entry hall and living room, as well as for the stair balusters. The motif on the etched stone insets within the ceiling coffers is hand-stenciled onto the linen chair backs. The bronze lantern reflects the ironwork tracery, while the antique baluster table pulls the warmth of the coffers into the center of the space.

The place cried out for the skills of a sympathetic architect, and ultimately help arrived from an unexpected quarter: the project's landscape architect, Garr Campbell. An older gentleman, broadly experienced, Garr had worked on lavishly scaled projects for the royal families of the Middle East (as well as for the Aga Khan in Paris), and had been engaged because of his knowledge of Islamic gardens and architecture, elements of which had been incorporated into the original house. Garr's understanding of the origins of the Mediterranean style, his grasp of the project's potential, and his enthusiasm and generosity as a collaborator enabled us to combine our abilities in a way that compensated for the absent team member.

Most of the house's original components had been erased by the Marble-eum and—though it had been inhabited by one of Utah's most prominent political families—no photographs of the original interiors existed. But I have always loved to do research, in this case into the not inconsiderable history of regional Mediterranean architecture; in complement, I've also always been a dedicated aesthetic sleuth, given to studying structures for clues to what they might have been. Thus our objective was to at once restore and detail the house, in a way that captured what I imagined to be the original architect's intentions, and to tease out the design's latent potential.

Though it is a design-writing cliché to say that the entry establishes the tone for what is to come, in this case it happens to be true. We wanted the space to make a grand statement but also a serene one; accordingly, the floor was finished in a soft gray limestone, and I based the exquisite pale-walnut ceiling on one in the Catalonian style I'd seen in a house by the renowned Florida architect Addison Mizner. Inspired by the ethos of Julia Morgan, architect of San Simeon, who famously designed every detail of her projects, I drew connections between the architectural and decorative elements; the motif in the limestone tile work was stenciled on the backs of the chairs, and carved into the plaster relief that surrounds the arched portal connecting the entry and the living room. In Salt Lake, I discovered one of the finest decorative ironwork companies in the United States, and engaged them to craft the staircase railing and the filigreed gates that can close off the portal (perhaps the world's fanciest pet-proofing). The overall effect foregrounds the craft and quality of material and detail that continues throughout the house, and is its hallmark.

As my handling of the entry suggests, my approach throughout was to highlight the original architecture's best qualities. In the living room, that meant applying ribs and medallions to the barrel-vaulted ceiling—so that now, everyone enthuses over what formerly went unnoticed. Previously, my clients' superlative art collection hadn't been displayed to proper advantage; in the dining room, by creating an arched niche specifically for a painting, I enabled the artwork to star. The garden room, once an underused porch, acknowledges the husband's love of fine woodwork with gutsy white oak paneling that's been bleached, wire-brushed, cerused—and allowed to crack. And I overcame my clients' desire to gut the paneled breakfast room, persuading them that if we erased the faux bois paint and finished it entirely in white, they'd discover how rejuvenating the space could be. (I also provided a sparkling, classically inspired mosaic floor.)

Did I put my "stamp" on the house? By working with Garr to give new life to an old classic, I'd like to think that we did the right thing—and in the process, created for the owners a refined refuge from their complex, busy life. If in fifty years, people look at our work and say, "Wow, they really knew how to build 'em in the old days," that will be "stamp" enough for me.

PREVIOUS PAGES: I added medallions and ribs to the living room's barrel-vaulted ceiling to give it more presence. My clients' Eurocentric furniture collection included a splendid Baroque mirror, which was undergirded with a muscular sofa and flanked with Baroque brackets. The room also received my collection's comfortable swooping club chairs and modern-patterned pillows. OPPOSITE: The portal leading to the dining room features elegantly turned ironwork and a relief sculpted from the plasterwork. A gilded Austrian chandelier hangs above eighteenth-century burled chairs.

ABOVE: To balance the dining room's architecture, which includes three archways, I added an arched niche, which displays one of my clients' finest artworks. OPPOSITE: The sconce is based on a design by Karl Friedrich Schinkel, and complements the Swedish Gustavian mirror and the French sideboard.

PREVIOUS PAGES: By erasing a dark faux bois paint job, I foregrounded the spectacular parabolic arched windows and doors of the breakfast room. I also added a sparkling mosaic floor and crowned the space with a delicate bronze lantern, with a glass smoke bell that mimics the room's shape. ABOVE AND OPPOSITE: An outdoor porch was enclosed to become a card room, and made gutsy via the cracked and wire-brushed paneling and the antique Belgian marble floor. No less robust are the beautifully carved antique Flemish mirror and Indian rosewood wardrobe (visible in the reflection), which I contrasted with more modern pieces, notably the wicker armchairs and the ottomans, which I designed to resemble Napoleon pastries.

The family room overlooks a cheerful patio with espaliered fruit trees. The furnishings are comfortable, upholstered in soft chenilles, and the light linen curtains feature a casual tattersall pattern. The coffee table, conversely, looks like it was made in a train yard to hold up a caboose. FOLLOWING PAGES: The family room also incorporates the kitchen, in which the crackled tile, ribbed glass, classic cabinetry, and icebox-style hardware speak to this historic home's 1930s origins.

RIGHT: The master suite is separated into sleeping and sitting zones by an arched portal. To increase the room's restfulness and subdue the sounds of the city, I custom-designed a dense silk and wool carpet and upholstered the walls in a sound-absorptive fabric, finishing the space in soft shades of blue, crème, and gray.
FOLLOWING PAGES, LEFT: I love to repurpose objects; for example, the lamp on the nightstand began life as a delicate Venetian candelabra.
FOLLOWING PAGES, RIGHT: The master bath's North African character was strengthened with the Islamic motif stenciled around the tub niche. The checkerboard marble is reflected elegantly in the polished-steel tub.

CALIFORNIA MODERN

had previously worked for the owners of this very unusual waterside residence in Southern California on a project that was more classic and traditional in character. But in fact, I am a great lover of modernism in its pure form—the Seagram Building and Lever House, which sit catty-corner to each other on Park Avenue, are two of my favorite examples of the style—and at Stanford, I studied under a protégé of Eero Saarinen, the modern architect known for the TWA Flight Center and the Gateway Arch. So I was well prepared for the opportunities this house presented.

What's more, my clients were special people. She was a successful psychologist and entrepreneur, and broadly knowledgeable regarding the applied arts. He had a decades-long involvement with fine architecture, having worked closely with Renzo Piano and Cesar Pelli on development projects, and enjoyed a personal and professional relationship with Isamu Noguchi, among many other renowned artists. As well, this man had an appreciation for the work of the great Mexican architect Luis Barragán, whose deceptively simple, planar forms—which seem to shape-shift in response to light—he found particularly well suited to the Southern California condition. In the 1960s, this gentleman arranged a meeting with Barragán, who sketched an idea for a house on the proverbial cocktail napkin—which the client then took to a local architect, who transformed this inspired wisp into reality. The house had turned out remarkably well, given its provenance, and my client was proud of it, and of the knowledge and inspiration he'd invested in its design.

By the time I got involved, however, the house faced challenges both temporal and architectural. After four decades, technology that once had been cutting-edge had grown antiquated, as had the methods by which the place had been built. Alterations had also been made in response to my client's extraordinary art collection: as the works got bigger, rooms were combined to accommodate them, until the plan—originally quite effective—lost track of its raison d'être. On balance, the house remained exceptional: a meaningful work, and an important representation of a particular place and time. But it needed to find its way to a new life.

We undertook a study of the available Barragán literature and, somewhat to my clients' surprise, I examined everything my predecessors had done and pulled together all of their best ideas; the owners assumed

I'd want to put my stamp on the place, but a great deal of aesthetic spadework existed, and I don't believe in change for the sake of change. In fact, the solution was evident: to simplify—indeed, clarify—the house, and make it a sublime container for the works by Matisse, Picasso, Mondrian, Frankenthaler, Léger, and other modern masters in the couple's collection. When doubts arose, I asked myself a simple question: What would Luis do?

The structure had been painted a variety of saturated colors that might be described as Barragán-esque, but my client and I believed the architect's genius lay in his manipulation of planes and volumes, so we chose to make the house entirely, purely white. I stripped and bleached all the floors; applied a new plaster finish to other surfaces; and created a large, oak-lined portal that acts as a frame between spaces—focusing the eye on such elements as the sculptural grand stair—and captures the mutable interplay of light and shadow as the interiors transform throughout the day. Many of the walls had rounded edges, and I squared them off, to give the transitions a crisp, simple flavor. Replacing the marble surround of the fireplace with concrete brought it into the house's presiding language, and attaching a long sitting platform allowed me to continue the planar experience while showcasing a pair of exquisite Giacometti works. I did everything I could to avoid compromising the architecture, even incorporating plaster sconces that seemed to emerge from the walls,

PREVIOUS PAGES: The simplicity of the interiors, coupled with the low-key luxury of the building materials, produced a gallery-like environment in which to showcase my clients' extraordinary art collection. As a single piquant decorative gesture, I introduced highly unusual plaster sconces, in the shape of floating floor lamps, which seem to emerge from the walls. OPPOSITE: A Mondrian painting is suspended above a simplified fireplace populated by iron rods. The Giacometti table reflects the sensuous sculptures and is surrounded by sleek leather chairs.

like discreet, abstract Robert Gober sculptures. The more we simplified, the greater the house felt like an object, a quiet white work of sculpture in and of itself, bathed in the California light.

One of my most consistent strategies, on every project, involves knitting the disparate elements of a room together with repeating visual motifs. This house afforded the opportunity to put this principle into practice in a unique way: I treated the place as a kind of architectural matryoshka doll, echoing the sculptural character of the larger residence in the forms of the furnishings and decorative elements. Hence the switchback curves of the Frank Gehry side chairs and the long, gentle crescent form of an Andrée Putman settee reflect the spiral staircase; the square volumes of upholstery and the Cubist dining table mirror the planar structure. The harborside location afforded me opportunities as well: while gold can seem garish in an urban setting, the warmth it draws from the reflected light of the cool water enabled me to accent the living room effectively with the material—to add jewelry to the spare serenity.

Of all the projects on which I've worked, this one might be the most elegant, thanks not to its modernity but rather its restraint. The place isn't a true Barragán, but I believe the master would approve—by returning the house to a condition of simplicity, I restored it to health and, I hope, a long life.

PREVIOUS PAGES: In the living room, I squared off the rectangular floor-to-ceiling windows that look out onto the garden's green wall. The rhythm they established—interspersed between paintings—brought an abstracted organic element into an otherwise pristine man-made environment. I designed the diamond-patterned carpet both to direct the eye and to softly echo the architectural furnishings, notably the Frank Gehry cardboard chairs sitting alongside the Matisse drawings and Barbara Hepworth bronze. The fireplace plays pedestal to a Giacometti pair (at left) and a Picasso ink drawing. RIGHT: An abundance of gold leaf glows with a lustrous beauty in the reflected waterside sunlight. The mirror also creates an alternate exterior view that contrasts with the portal beside it.

In the master bedroom, overlooking Newport's harbor, my client requested that I retain the Savonnerie carpet, a beloved vestige of an earlier life that might have been at odds with the décor's newly modernized character. By carefully considering the room's other components—the color palette and, in particular, the forms and silhouettes—I was able to honor his request without disrupting the spirit of the new design.

ABOVE: To light the kitchen, I brought in an unusual track system that is suspended just below the beams—a quotidian element reconceived as a sculptural art piece. Restrained lacquer cabinets, glass counters, and open shelving direct the eye to the great room beyond. OPPOSITE AND FOLLOWING PAGES: The pool house was redesigned to bring its language into conformity with that of the main house. The grid form creates a brise-soleil while reinforcing the architectural connection.

THE EMBRACEABLE HOME

St. Louis has one of the largest repositories of fine residential architecture in the United States, a trove dating from the beginning of the twentieth century. This house, in the city's estate district, an area of rolling land surrounding a country club, is representative of that age of quality. Built in the prewar years, the residence might look as if it belongs in Connecticut, but its particular Midwestern character arises from a freewheeling hybridization of styles: paired with the New England neoclassicism are beautiful overhanging eaves that belong to the Arts and Crafts genre. As a destination for émigré German and Italian artisans in the nineteenth century, St. Louis also enjoys a craft tradition, evident in the house's carefully finished brickwork and interior details. The residence exuded an inbuilt modesty, the product of a time when it was assumed that a comfortable, practical American family house would be well designed and soundly constructed, simply as a matter of pride. The place had suffered a bit over the decades, from bad additions and wear and tear. But its essential character and integrity remained—unshaken, and unshakeable.

At the same time, my clients were very modern and, indeed, leading-edge in their tastes and interests, and it felt important to me to keep up with them, to do the unexpected. Accordingly, my work proceeded on parallel tracks: correcting the architectural miscues while staying true to the overall quality, and designing interiors for daily living that conveyed a certain panache.

The living room reflects my design scheme's overall balance of livability, sophistication, and surprise. The trio of portals leading to the dining room, sunroom, and study were quite low, but each was crowned by a superbly carved classical frieze, which we painted white to give the space more height, and to celebrate these splendid original flourishes. The walls, by contrast, were stenciled and glazed a highly reflective shade of tobacco that enriches the room and envelops visitors, while the glossy white ceiling captures and holds the light. Within this setting, my clients freed me to do what, in my own estimation, I do best: create custom-designed, elegantly tailored upholstered pieces, irresistibly comfortable and with graceful modern silhouettes, that extract the starch from the architecture and make the room a warm gathering place for any time of day or occasion.

The dining room continues the design scheme but shifts its direction. My clients are passionate about English antiques, and this space is a showcase for them: a Hepplewhite table and a handsomely scaled and proportioned Sheraton sideboard accompany my custom-designed Regency-style chairs. Yet my experience with different aesthetic periods has taught me how well, if sometimes unexpectedly, certain movements partner one another. Here, I was able to draw in a Deco-era Murano glass chandelier and contemporaneous starburst sconces that proved to be entirely in character. With the reflective walls subtly transitioning from blue to green—from heaven to earth—and a surprising, almost tribal patterned fabric on the chairs, the room reinforced my clients' desires and expectations even as it vitalized them.

I have always been a great fan of English country-house design as practiced by such legends as Nancy Lancaster and John Fowler; their ability to alchemize an understated charm into the acme of timeless style reminds me that "interior decoration" is an art form worthy of the closest consideration and respect. My desire to reinterpret the Lancaster-Fowler sensibility for a new era found a nesting place in the house's library, which also serves as the wife's study. I like contrasting textures in rooms, and patterns as well, as the small, medium, and large repeats in the wallpaper, curtains, and carpet suggest. Opposite a French coffee table from the 1950s, I placed a splendid Regency rosewood desk, paired with a gilded eighteenth-century chair that is as comfortable as it is stylish. Certain of the fabrics here are embroidered rather than printed, and the majolica stool and floral curtains make a classic connection to the adjoining garden (originally designed by the great English garden maestro Russell Page)—even as the hand-hammered square nickel curtain rod and rings tug the room back into modernity.

Many clients prefer not to veer too far from tradition, the aesthetic world in which they grew up. While this couple had a strong attachment to the familiar, they enjoyed being knocked slightly, pleasantly off-stride by their home's design, an experience to which they continue to contribute with regular infusions of newly collected objects and artworks—which always seem to comfortably adapt. "Taste is realizing the essence of a place" is one of Nancy Lancaster's great observations. In this house, that essence was both the historical character of a fine work of architecture and the soul and spirit of a family's life.

PREVIOUS PAGES: A view from the living room into the library reveals one of the three classical friezes that were original to the space. A pair of black-lacquered Biedermeier chests, beneath vintage mercury-glass mirrors, flank the portal. OPPOSITE: I designed the dining chairs, based on an English Regency model, to complement the antique dining table, and commissioned a high-gloss "abstract landscape," which shades from blue above to green below, for the walls.

PREVIOUS PAGES: The living room opens onto the dining room (left) and sunroom (right). Tobacco-colored walls increase the room's warmth and intimacy, while the glossy white crown molding and ceiling make the room feel taller and capture the light. I created the upholstered pieces, with their elegant profiles, for maximum comfort. RIGHT: The library, which updates the warmth of the classic English decorating style associated with Lancaster and Fowler, overlooks a garden originally designed by Russell Page. I paired a gilded eighteenth-century armchair with a Regency rosewood desk; the table is 1950s French. FOLLOWING PAGES: Custom corner cabinets and a marble mosaic floor give the sunroom the flavor of a conservatory. The chandelier, which combines porcelain and iron, is 1950s French; the plant stands, with their lively cartouches, are late nineteenth century and were found in a château in Sweden.

The ultra-comfortable family room is swathed in layers of fabric, including one affixed to the walls. I designed the oval-shaped side tables to support the room's clubby elegance, but balanced them with a more relaxed bi-level oak-slatted coffee table reminiscent of an old lobster trap.

CABO HACIENDA

Having the opportunity to design a home overlooking the Sea of Cortés in Mexico—the first time I'd ever worked in the country—was a great gift. To study the history of Mexican architecture, to delve into the building culture and grapple with the special challenges it presented, taught me many things—lessons I will always cherish, along with my memories of the land and its people.

My clients had purchased a lot in a new community that sat between the sea and the desert, where the marine breezes blended with the sharp aromas of the landscape, all beneath a brilliant sky. Their choice had been thoughtful: Most of the properties were cheek by jowl with one another and had restricted views. My clients, however, had picked one on a high promontory, and the 270-degree panorama embraced the water, distant mountains, and desert.

When I spoke to the community's mandarins about their aesthetic guidelines, I was informed that they wanted their Baja seaside resort to resemble an Italian hill town. While this struck me as counterintuitive, my clients' property did, in fact, occupy the high ground. My clients had tasked me with handling the architecture as well as the interiors. And so, not wanting to do a bad pastiche, I traveled to Italy—to the Veneto, the land of Palladio's villas—in search of knowledge and inspiration.

Experiencing some of the maestro's creations in person and in context—notably Villa Barbaro and Villa Emo—was transformative. Emo's two arcaded, symmetrical *barchesse*, agricultural structures on which Palladio had bestowed elegance and dignity, found their way into the courtyard design of my project. Returning from Italy with my imagination aflame, I stopped off in California to refresh my understanding of the Mediterranean Revival style, for the ease and originality with which it absorbs multiple influences (I borrowed from a Santa Barbara municipal building for my clients' bell tower). To keep things surprising, I also drew on the design of the central loggia of The Breakers, Richard Morris Hunt's late-nineteenth-century Vanderbilt mansion in Newport.

In the end, my frequent collaborator, architect Stephen Morgan, and I came up with a house that combined two cultures: on the one hand, a palazzo that would have seemed entirely at home atop an Italian hill;

on the other, a typical Mexican hacienda constructed around a central court. In the spirit of the adventure, and in homage to its esteemed models, the clients gave our creation a name: Casa Verdad—the house of truth.

The form of the house is simple, axial, and layered. Entering from a forecourt, one passes through a bell tower with a chamfered top (and an actual, ringable bell) into the expansive enclosed courtyard, with a fountain at its center; directly beyond it, flanked by the dining room on one side and the master suite on the other, lies the open-air colonnaded loggia that forms the living room and overlooks the pool and the sea. On either side of the courtyard are the house's two linear wings, one given to the kitchen, family room, study, and a guest suite, the other containing the remaining bedrooms and baths. Though the house consumes virtually the entire lot, it doesn't feel cramped: without are the unobstructed views, while within, nearly all the rooms overlook the courtyard. And though Casa Verdad remains distinctly Italianate when seen from below, once you traverse the campanile, there's no mistaking the presence of Mexico.

Though I strove to shape rooms that were neither overwhelming nor out of proportion, the house also evinces an unmistakable sense of grandeur—it's a one-story structure, but in some places, the ceilings reach a height of twenty-five feet. Since the architecture is so spectacular and the view conversation-stopping,

ABOVE: The tall glass-paneled cabinets (which we back-painted turquoise) reinforce the kitchen's verticality, while the pyramidal figure in the carved wood lower cabinetry abstracts a ubiquitous Mexican geometric form. OPPOSITE: We used textural woven abaca furniture throughout the house. The dining room features five chandeliers: an ironwork form of barrel staves crafted locally, and four Moroccan lanterns.

I kept the furniture simple, notably the wonderfully textural, handwoven hemp seating elements. We also had fun with the decoration, which reflects Mexico's pancultural traditions. You'll find the influence of Morocco, Japan, Indonesia, and the Middle East, as well as the better-known presence of Spain, and—with some strong Italian seasoning—we drew upon them all.

Mexico is justly renowned for its craftwork, and as with most countries that excel at the applied arts, different regions have different specialties. Determined to draw on this resource, and to get it right, I traveled around the country—to San Miguel de Allende, Cuernavaca, Guadalajara, and many lesser-known towns—to seek out the finest artisans and explain what I had in mind. Mexican traditions include beautiful plasterwork, painted finishes, and pebbled floors, and the country's artisans are especially adept at using stenciling to articulate architectural elements like windows, doors, and wainscoting; examples can be found throughout the house. We engaged skilled ironworkers to create railings, gates, and lanterns, and installed meticulously crafted hammered-tin doors behind the bed in the master suite, which the couple can open to expose their bath to the water view.

Sometimes the results of collaboration were a surprise. For the loggia, I designed a mantelpiece in the Italian style, complete with acanthus leaves and cartouches, handed over my plans to the artisans—and got back a version of it that was a mixture of Indian, Mayan, and Baroque. Initially I was stunned, until I admitted how incredibly well the piece had turned out, and how well suited it was to the overall scheme. That's the whole point of working with craftspeople. As a designer, I can have a vision. But it is the *interpretation* of that vision that gives my design its authenticity—its sense of place—and its strength.

This project was, in every sense, one from the heart. I enjoyed every aspect of its creation, and especially loved working with the local people, and those from across the nation, who brought the house into existence. The Mexicans, I noticed, say yes to every request, even the ones they're not certain they can pull off. I found them to be very positive, very gentle, and that soul and spirit permeate every part of my clients' home—and that, I promise, is the *verdad*.

OPPOSITE: The master suite's entry reveals the Mexican traditions of superlative plasterwork and stenciling, which use decoration to define space architecturally. A Moroccan silver fountain continues the motif of water from the exterior rooms and provides a gentle overlay of white noise. The candle niches flanking the fountain are lined with reflective mother-of-pearl, and the pierced brass lanterns above provide enhancing romantic light. FOLLOWING PAGES: The hammered-tin doors behind the custom bed in the master suite, both executed by local artisans from my designs, open onto the master bath, enabling my clients to look out to the water view. A seventeenth-century Spanish chest houses the TV and looks as though it was salvaged from a sunken Catalonian galleon.

A SWEDISH JOURNEY

When I was a small child, my parents engaged a Swedish nanny named Lilly, whose duty it was to see to my care. There were two incredibly rambunctious older boys in the house, and Lilly's arrival enabled my overtaxed mother to set me to one side, as it were, and put her focus on them. Consequently, Lilly and I became very close—she loved me as though I were her own, and I returned her affection unreservedly. And yet she was very Swedish: on the one hand proper and severe, and on the other emotional in ways that seemed strange to us. None of us entirely understood her, yet despite this Ingmar Bergman-meets-Kansas City setup, my parents knew I would have been devastated if she'd gone. And so on Lilly stayed, and we remained close until the end of her life—when, at our last meeting, I shook her hand, knowing that I couldn't throw my arms around her. For many years afterward, I nursed a desire to work in Sweden, to immerse myself in the culture so as to better understand this woman who, despite her opacity, had been like a mother to me.

Eventually, I got my wish. I was introduced to a couple—he is American, she is Swedish by birth—who'd purchased several properties on Värmdö, the largest island in the Stockholm archipelago, a landscape of large granite outcroppings and pale-green forests that erupt with wildflowers in summer. There were a handful of twentieth-century structures, all very classic in style, and this couple wanted to transform them into an aesthetically consistent compound, to which they and their children could travel from America in the warm months for a traditional "old country" experience.

There has been a great resurgence of enthusiasm for postwar Scandinavian furniture, and a simultaneous abeyance of interest (and consequent drop in price) in Gustavian antiques. This represented a singular opportunity: I explained to my clients that if they wanted a romantic retreat in the classical tradition, it was to the seventeenth and eighteenth centuries they should be looking—and the wisest course would be for me to go to Sweden, travel the country, and economically put together a collection of antique furniture. To this, they generously agreed—and I was off on a voyage of discovery at once professional and personal.

PREVIOUS PAGES: To establish a Swedish country tone immediately, I used colors infused with gray blues, spare yet pretty antique furniture, and hand-loomed Scandinavian runners. The stair in this guesthouse combines motifs I saw on the exteriors of various country houses and in Scandinavian pattern books. LEFT: The shapely profile of the marble lamp echoes the lines of the Rococo tea table. OPPOSITE: The pine floorboards were very white when they arrived, so I infused them with a slightly gray stain, and waxed them to achieve a "scrubbed lye" effect. In pursuit of elegant simplicity, I kept furnishings to a minimum and selected ones with graceful silhouettes, such as the Rococo clock and the eighteenth-century German table.

The days developed a pattern: I'd be picked up by an antiques dealer, and we'd drive for hours in a supremely awkward silence (interrupted, periodically, by my attempts to chat in pidgin Swedish) to Småland or Dalarna, regions in which the great furniture warehouses could be found, or else we'd visit forlorn palaces and castles—places so cold you could see your breath—where dusty drop cloths would be drawn back and long-forgotten treasures revealed. It was a particularly personal immersion in a national sensibility, one that (along with the craft-based construction process) taught me much about how the people I encountered worked, felt, and lived. I collected volumes about Swedish country style, and visited as many relevant places as I could, including Skansen, Stockholm's remarkable outdoor museum of vernacular buildings. By the time I'd built my clients' collection, I had an understanding of the project that was not only well schooled but instinctive and, of course, emotional.

The first of the buildings I undertook, the guesthouse, established the project's character. We began by gutting the uninspiring structure and fitting it with elements drawn from Sweden's residential heritage: bleached wide-plank pine floors (limed a light gray), simple moldings, and a staircase whose silhouette conflated craft elements I'd seen in, and on, different houses. Columns dating from the 1920s were inserted to give definition to two adjoining rooms. Colors were chosen for their responsiveness to the soft, granular northern light. I replaced all the doors with Sweden's ubiquitous multipaneled, knotty-pine variety, waxed rather than painted to showcase their simplicity and character.

This simple palette served as the background for the silhouettes of the furniture and objects, which—even at their most refined, like the daybed in the entry hall—were playful, even folklike, rather than formal. In the rugs, curtains, and upholstery, I used more patterning than the average Swede would accept, but I kept them quiet. Decorative objects, like copperware and plates, were spare and also functional. There is no Swedish word for *tchotchke*.

Though somewhat more grand and colorful, the main house drew on the same essentially modest, folk-based sensibility. Two preexisting, rather serious columns flank the portal between the foyer and entry hall, the ceiling of which received a reflective, high-gloss treatment to capture more light; but the country-crafted stair rail is a cousin to the one in the guest cottage, and the layered fabrics that borrow folkloric patterns are executed in traditional needlework techniques. Perhaps the most representative space is the combined kitchen and dining room, which remains at once dramatic and everyday. The centerpiece is a fourteen-foot-long dining table, my design for which draws on simple farm furniture, executed in reclaimed wood. I left the slatted pine ceiling raw, but gave the boards a lively multidirectional treatment. There are floor-to-ceiling patterned curtains that bestow a certain stately grandeur, and a hand-scraped cupboard and dresser. This room encourages the traditional, and cherished, social rituals of Swedish life in general, and this family in particular—at every meal, every seat at the table is taken, and company is savored to the fullest.

When I was eighteen, I spent a year as an exchange student living with a family in Denmark, which taught me not to compare everything to the way it was back home (and find it "less than") but to embrace, and celebrate, the differences. That was my objective with this project: to write a script for a romantic Swedish summer, to which the family could submit itself utterly. And today, even though the kids are now college-aged and itching to cut the cord, they still want to return to their summer idyll—to forget that they're Americans for a time, and participate in their mother's, and indeed their own, heritage.

I never let on to my clients, or even my staff, that this journey was personal as well as professional. But when it was over, I did feel that the veil of difference between Lilly and myself had been lifted. What had seemed strange made sense; I understood her reserve, and the great depth of emotion beneath it. My clients had found their way home, and so had I.

PREVIOUS PAGES: As the two tables, the chest of drawers, and the settee reveal, Swedish dealers hand-scrape their antiques down to the original finish, leaving them beautifully textured and patinated. OPPOSITE: Midsummer light filtered through birches outside is caught by the brass Danish kerosene chandelier and the sheer linen curtains.

ABOVE: In the country, Swedes tend to display their china. I also designed the rack in the kitchen to facilitate the farm tradition of taking down your own plate at mealtimes.
OPPOSITE: A Gustavian sofa bed anchors the guesthouse entry hall. Though influenced by the formal Louis XVI style, the backboard's carving represents more of a Swedish folk treatment.

PREVIOUS PAGES: The Swedes favor simple textiles and carpets with discreet patterns, and the bedrooms follow their lead. All the doors were found in the local version of Home Depot: plain, three-paneled Swedish pine, requiring nothing more than a coat of wax. RIGHT: As the main house backs up to a granite cliff, it was important to bring in as much light as possible on the other side—hence the entry's glossy ceiling. I dug up a seventeenth-century baker's table to balance the weight of the columns, and designed a Swedish interpretation of formal balusters for the stair rail. The "Dalarna red" hue is picked up in the demilune tables and embroidered strawberries on the curtains. FOLLOWING PAGES: The dining room revolves around a fourteen-foot-long table of my design, based on a traditional local farm typology. (I found the fourteen Rococo chairs in the rafters of an old glass factory.) The carpet is inspired by the weave of Scandinavian sweaters, and curtains with needlework reminiscent of country samplers add warmth.

ABOVE: Though Austrian, the writing chest appealed to my clients'
folkloric sensibility. OPPOSITE: Beneath a canvas cover in a cold manor
house, I discovered the impressive neoclassical cupboard.

OPPOSITE AND ABOVE: The house features high gables and a steep roof, and when I first saw the attic space that became the master bedroom, the drama of its form was concealed beneath a coat of white paint. To break the room down into dramatic shapes, I added paneling upholstered in an embroidered Danish cotton. The soft green hue suggests the dappled birches outside the window.

ABOVE: The former barn, painted "Falu red," nestles under birches beside a pond. OPPOSITE: The barn's "celebration" room represents a form of Scandinavian repatriation. Remarkably, it is difficult to find reclaimed wood in Sweden, as the people tend not to demolish their vernacular buildings. So all of the wood in this room—a mix of everything from walnut to pine, and all hewn by Norwegian farmers in Wisconsin—was imported from the United States. Country shutters close off the cruel winter drafts. The antique brick floor came from Poland.

PALM BEACH CHIC

This homeowner asked us to emblazon HELLO, DAHLING on her welcome mat.

How can you not embrace the wonderfully cheeky ostentation of Palm Beach? With enormous manicured hedges surrounding French châteaux and Italian palazzi, there is a disorienting juxtaposition of over-the-top formality and an extremely informal climate. Similarly, the residents really put on the dog, but there's a sense of humor to it, a chic, Slim Aarons–style lightness to go with the Lilly Pulitzer and the helmet hair. This duality carries over into the decorative milieu, which can swing from an elevated northern elegance dipped in white to colors that were not made by God. It is a land unto itself. And, always, a celebration.

Having expressed my affection, I must quickly add that there is a difference between cheekiness and frivolity, an important distinction for the design direction of this project. My clients had purchased a residence in the Louis XVI style, a *serious* house that conveyed a sense of darkness. They wanted precisely the opposite, something formal but fresh-feeling: a house that derived its esprit from a wide-ranging design intelligence, married to a tongue-in-cheek flair suited to entertaining and having fun—Noël Coward, updated to the twenty-first century. I was entirely in accord.

The entryway immediately establishes the tone, and with a minimum of elements. The space has a certain inherent drama, with a stair sweeping up to the second floor, and a large portal that opens into the living room. I wanted neither to compete with nor be overwhelmed by the architecture. And so we painted the walls a deep rich yellow (a favorite of the husband's); unrolled a beautifully patterned and textured sisal carpet; hung a simple white plaster chandelier in the style of Giacometti; and installed a single, sculptural klismos chair, improbably wrapped in snakeskin. The design's Orientalism presents a spare sophistication—and the off-kilter knock of the snakeskin reminds you not to take the place, or yourself, too seriously.

For the living room's influences, I mined Palm Beach history. If you stroll down Worth Avenue, you'll see North African–style latticework windows, carved from marble, designed by the seminal south Florida architect Addison Mizner, whose Mediterranean Revival works give the city its indelible character. With these in mind, I

PREVIOUS PAGES: The loggia of this Palm Beach residence, just off the living room, reflects the decoration's quality of carefree, slightly tongue-in-cheek elegance—especially the oversize, spirit-of-Slim-Aarons curtains, the bold graphic color, and the bamboo garden stools. RIGHT: The broad portal connecting the foyer and the living room is flanked by a very Palm Beach snakeskin-wrapped klismos chair (cheeky, unless you're the snake) and a Chinese porcelain urn. The latter finds its way into the living room via the figure in the carpet, which abstracts motifs from Asian decorative objects; the contrasting Greek key border corrals the carpet with formality.

OPPOSITE AND RIGHT: The living room incorporates a multiplicity of patterned elements, including marquetry occasional tables, fabrics, moldings, and decorative Neptunian elements such as coral, sand dollars, and starfish. I held these elements in balance with a consistent color ground of pale blues and crèmes, by alternating patterns with solids, and by repeating motifs–the Greek key carpet border also appears on the sofa pillow as well as the lampshades, and the blue-and-white chair fabric turns up again in the Roman shades.

mixed Moroccan and Indian elements—a latticework marble coffee table and marquetry cabinet executed in ivory, bone-inlay side tables, and colorful patterned fabrics—with a surprisingly sympathetic Adirondack-style mantelpiece mirror. (The white plaster sconces in the shape of horseshoe crabs are, conversely, from the School of Gabor.) There are other salutes to Palm Beach: the "frog" fasteners on the back of the custom-designed club chair are a dressmaker detail, the sort of thing you'd see in town on a Chanel jacket, and the large framed panel of hand-painted Chinese wallpaper recalls the very formal style of the past. The room is a bazaar of influences; but their number is limited, and they are held together by the Palm Beach sensibility and the repeating shades of blue, which make the living room feel as cool and refreshing as a dip in the pool.

I don't think of my work as "eclectic," and in fact the word can be synonymous with "mishmash." Yet "eclectic" might well be applied to the house's dining room, the centerpiece of which is a large Indian birdcage that we repurposed into a chandelier and hung over the modern rectilinear wood table. You will also find in the mix gigantic blue-and-white Chinese urns on Art Deco pedestals; Moroccan plates hung on the bright yellow walls around a French Régence cabinet; and big, comfortable rattan chairs. Yet the room is surprisingly quiet–I dislike visual noise–as I have maintained a soothing consistency of tonalities: many of the elements are in a shade of

The living room includes elements that recall the formality of the past: the framed panels of hand-painted Gracie wallpaper flanking the Italian fireplace, for example, and the Fortuny-style chandelier. But the décor is offbeat as well, a whimsy reflected in the plaster "horseshoe crab" sconces, the Adirondack-style mirror, the *mashrabiya* marble coffee table, and the "frog" clips on the back of the bergère—a couture detail very much in keeping with the local spirit.

PREVIOUS PAGES, LEFT: A silver pheasant from the 1950s struts toward a most upset rooster on the table. PREVIOUS PAGES, RIGHT: In the dining room, I indulged my clients' love of blue-and-white porcelain with the Chinese urns and decorative plates. As in the living room, the repetition of textures, colors, and forms holds in balance a cornucopia of elements, including a chandelier made from a birdcage. LEFT: On the second floor, the ceiling was two feet lower than on the floor below, so we used tall curtains and a four-poster with a high top to create a sense of height in the master bedroom. The artwork above the headboard gently brings in the ocean, as do the soft embroidered curtains, which introduce the soothing green-and-blue color scheme.

THE ART OF ELEGANCE   133

caramel (there's even a suggestion of it in the walls), and white repeats in the carpet, curtains, plates, and chandelier. There is also a harmonious interplay of forms; for example, the curve of the chair arms and the flourishes on the birdcage above them. The connections are subtle, and not accidental—they enabled me to pull together the multiple elements in a way that avoids the "eclectic" curse, and invests the room with a connoisseur's consistency.

One of my favorite spaces in the house is the study, as it reinterprets one of the town's signature style cues: animal-print fabric. Rather than put a faux zebra or leopard skin on the walls, I found a vital but discreet ikat textile that abstracts an animal hide, and brought in a bolder variant of it for a pair of traditional American wing chairs. The carpet is monochrome but textured, and the more tribal components are balanced by the modern ottoman and lamp, bronze side tables, and, not least, an acrylic desk that's stylish and unusual enough to qualify as a vintage piece. The room is witty, and very much a participant in the local visual culture. The specificity of the choices—the idea of reinterpretation—makes it feel timeless.

As Noël Coward might have noted about his own work, being simultaneously cheeky and stylish, and making it all seem effortless, is the objective. This is not, however, so easily done. It is my hope that with this project, I've been Cowardly in the best sense.

One of my favorite rooms in the house is the office,
where I used an ostrich leather-clad acrylic
desk and strongly patterned ikat fabrics to evoke
the long-standing Palm Beach penchant for
animal skins. The rather striking starburst mirror
between the windows pays it all off.

THE ART OF ELEGANCE   137

LA DOLCE VITA

may be the only Midwesterner in history whose initial reaction, upon first seeing the promised land of California, was disappointment. You see, I was raised in Kansas City, in a lushly green part of town; when I arrived in Palo Alto for my first semester at Stanford, all I could think was, "Why is everything so *brown*?" (I didn't realize that autumn is the driest time of year.) But it was the scent that saved me—the pungent perfume that seems so particular to California. Inhaling that earthy aroma, I felt at home.

Over the next four years, I explored the state, developing a particular fondness for the Bay Area, which still had that Barbary Coast spirit about it. Best of all were the weekends spent biking around the wine country, after which my friends and I would make our way to Valhalla, a restaurant owned by an ex-madam who'd become the mayor of Sausalito. Rolling through Napa and Sonoma, you thought there could be no place on earth more beautiful. If America is God's country, the California vineyard region is where he makes love.

All this was in my mind when I was asked to design a getaway for a longtime client and her husband amidst the vineyards of Northern California. My client had never lived in the West. But this woman's adult children wound up in the Bay Area, and her husband had previously owned a place in Napa, where he'd kept a vineyard; so the couple purchased a hilltop retreat, which they saw in part as a place to gather together family and friends, but also to spend time alone and savor the area's particular dolce vita.

The house they'd found had been built by a family of winemakers, and showed a strong Provençal influence. That region's vernacular architecture is rugged, with buildings made of stone and plaster and crowned by distinctive terra-cotta tile roofs, and that same rough elegance distinguished my clients' new home. Within its massive walls, it featured a cornucopia of attractive elements: muscular beams, limestone floors, rough-hewn doors, and low-slung side porches that kept the heat of the day at bay. The cumulative effect was romantic, and my clients had enhanced the narrative by adding a pair of picturesque guest cottages designed by the New York architect Alan Wanzenberg, styled to resemble agricultural sheds.

Even more evocative than the residence itself—and a formative influence on my design strategy—was the site. The house sat atop what we in the East would describe as a mountain, and what the area's residents call

a hill. There are magnificent views; a reservoir surrounded by virgin land down below; and slopes dense with ancient, craggy oak trees. Behind the house, one finds a small vineyard (that produces phenomenal wine). But it's those indelible California aromas—santolina, lavender, sage, bay, jasmine, eucalyptus—that most influence the property's character. And somehow the aroma is reflected in the palette: the brownish green of the flora, the chalky white of the dry, crumbling soil.

Crisp modern jewel tones, I realized, would be entirely out of place, and it made no sense to add elements that lacked texture. The objective was a simple California Mediterranean elegance, unpretentious yet refined: a home that would have suited people who'd rather have a few well-made things than a house full of finery.

The finishes were essential to the design's success. Together we worked on developing the character of the wood, in particular the overscaled beams: though it was reclaimed, the material had to be cut and finished—stained, textured, and wire-brushed—to reflect the spirit of the house. The floors, too, were thoughtfully treated, hand-smoked to a shade of gray, and then waxed. Mottled plaster walls were infused with pigment rather than painted, and the ironwork hardware revealed a more contemporary sensibility, lean and industrial yet entirely in sympathy with the timeworn limestone, troweled plaster, and wood beams.

RIGHT: The artisanal upholstery in the living area (which adjoins the dining space) is composed primarily of textured linens and raw cottons in related shades of beige, camel, caramel, and crème. The iron doors open to a view of the reservoir below. FOLLOWING PAGES: The dining chairs are decorated with Provençal-style embroidery and fitted loosely, as though stitched together by the wives and sisters of the vineyard workers. The stone floor anchors the double-height room and holds its own against wood-paneled screens.

We converted a garage into a family room, finishing the walls in a vertical paneling treated to resemble reclaimed barn wood overpainted with many layers of milk paint. (The beams are *actual* reclaimed barn wood.) Above the Norwegian bench settle, I hung an arrangement of pages from a book featuring dried pressed flowers, recalling the botanist Carl Linnaeus, who papered an entire room in his home with botanical drawings.
FOLLOWING PAGES: The family room also draws comfort from a contemporary American cloth rug, an antique Swedish Mora clock, and a raffia-wrapped Italian chair.

My clients wanted to sustain a degree of simplicity in all of the project's facets, so we avoided the elaborate furniture that often turns up in wine-country villas. Instead, we chose items like weathered interior doors; an antique French armoire that over time had shed its paint; tables and chairs with simple, beautiful lines textured by the flaws of age—objects that had enjoyed the appreciation of their owners throughout their lives. Slipcovers that drape onto the floor were made from rough linens and burlaps, with the sort of simple country crewelwork that might have been done by the vineyard workers when they weren't crushing grapes.

Certain of my design principles remain evident in the furniture arrangements, particularly in the public rooms. I always want the seating to "converse," so the sofa is flanked by chairs; ottomans have been included for versatility; a smaller grouping has been arranged by the fireplace; and there's a mix of firmer, upright seating and deep upholstery. Women and men, I have observed, tend to gravitate toward different kinds of chairs: women prefer armless ones that enable them to perch, whereas men are happy to drop into something that swallows them up. Each gesture and grouping serves, individually and collectively, to invite people in.

While I don't like my rooms to look consciously "decorated," neither do I want them to seem ill-considered. Here, the living room has repeating visual cues in the form of colors and materials—beige, caramel, camel, off-white, and the frequent use of ironwork—that hold the space together and give it coherence. Though there can be a relaxed, casual quality to a space (and in this house, there *should* be), maintaining a tightly pulled together scheme gives the room a sense of readiness, even occasion. Combining the two conditions makes every moment of the life within a home, even the little ones, memorable.

In each project I create, I endeavor to bring something personal to the work, to find a way into the design that—though the house belongs to my clients—enables me to draw on my own knowledge and experiences. In this case, the emotional and visual memories of my university years, the rough majesty of the land, and most of all a deep awareness of Northern California life when it was still overlain with heedless innocence found their way into every aspect of this home. All helped to imbue it with the kind of refined elegance that, I believe, typifies our work.

And: it's pretty. I am *not* afraid of pretty.

Adjacent to the master bedroom is a two-sided chaise (designed by my studio) for comfortable morning reading. The home office beyond conceals its technology entirely in the glass-fronted armoire against the back wall.

The textures of the master bedroom—olive-toned crewelwork, weathered leather, iron doors, the mottled silk carpet, the waxed lemon wood bed, and the sheer blue linen curtains—would evoke a sense of romance even if you didn't look out at the stunning mountain view.

This alfresco dining porch is softened by the reclaimed beams, terra-cotta, and mustard seed plaster. A simple farm table and outdoor bistro chairs finish the story (helped along by sunflowers and a bottle of the local vintage).

While the main house and the guesthouses convey the character of nineteenth-century vernacular buildings, the introduction of steel-frame windows and doors—a California tradition dating from the interwar years—enlarges the project's historical narrative. Soft sheers, a ribbed carpet, and slipcovered upholstery welcome the weary.

ABOVE AND OPPOSITE: Pale raspberry and buttercream infuse
these bedrooms with an airy romance. Custom embroidered pillows,
headboards, and coverlets enhance the aura of the vineyard.

POOLSIDE PAVILION

have always held that everyone has taste, and it is my task to use every tool in my interior designer's kit to clarify my clients' own taste. The owners of this classic 1920s St. Louis property are a case in point. Some time after I'd completed the renovation of the main residence, they decided to put in a pool and construct a pool house. The pair hired a local architect—a good one—and described what they had in mind, but these wishes transformed, on the drawing board, into something distinctly postmodern in flavor. Although it was the popular style of the time, the couple sensed that it was out of sync with their Georgian mansion; though they didn't have the architectural language to express what they felt, their instincts were spot on, and I set about rethinking the project.

I was able to draw inspiration for both the principal façade and the plan from two sources. The first was the magnificent Georgian rear elevation of the main house itself, beautifully carved in Indiana limestone by one of old St. Louis's transplanted Italian artisans. My second inspiration was a little pavilion that the great Elsie de Wolfe designed, discreetly hidden behind the *hôtel particulier* she maintained in Versailles before the Second World War. The outcome was a tripartite structure: a great room with a façade related to the house, flanked by two smaller brick-clad, trellised wings containing the changing rooms and kitchen.

On the pool house's exterior, I replicated the Masonic iconography that appeared on the house's façade, and borrowed the proportions from the entry, combining it with a low-pitched roof finished with slate tiles identical to those on the house. I also designed a metal railing for the roof; I call it an "ice screen"—as in, something to keep the ice from falling off the roof in winter—but it's primarily a decorative flourish meant to accentuate the elegant horizontality of the roof. I also inserted three large arched doorways, rising to nearly ten feet, aligned on both sides of the structure, as an antidote to the hot Midwestern summers: my clients throw them open, and cooling cross-breezes flow through the interior.

When the pavilion was completed, my clients were pleased that I was able to interpret their taste, and continued a relationship with me that has now lasted two decades and embraced multiple projects. It was *my* instinct, when we first met, that it was (as the saying goes) the beginning of a beautiful friendship—and so it has proven to be.

PREVIOUS PAGES: My design for this pool house, on the grounds of a classic 1920s St. Louis home, draws on two principal inspirations: the commanding Georgian limestone elevation of the house itself, and the prewar pavilion Elsie de Wolfe designed for herself in a sleepy French suburb called Versailles. RIGHT: In contrast to the dramatic formal exterior, the large room at the structure's center is clad in horizontal boards of glazed poplar, which are as lively and varied as brushstrokes. The dining chairs wear slipcovers cut from thick terry-cloth towels, for which I designed and stitched a family monogram crest. The comfortable banquette, designed to accommodate wet bathing suits, plays host to the family's exuberant young swimmers. The dolphin jardinières gracefully reference the water spirits, while the cool limestone floor provides a respite from the searing summer heat.

ABOVE AND OPPOSITE: The great room is flanked on one side by changing rooms and on the other by a kitchen. The casual air is slightly contravened by the formality of the floor and the robust classical casing surrounding the door.

BAHAMIAN PARADISE

This house, a vacation getaway in the Bahamas for a large Midwestern family, presented me with one of the most intriguing design challenges I've yet to face: that of translating a highly specific, and specifically *regional*, way of life into an idiom suited to a very different locale—without losing its essence.

My clients are immensely vital, athletic people—they grab life head-on. She has a wonderfully self-deprecating sense of humor; they both like to party and tell stories, and have a weakness for fun, silly things. These frequent travelers enjoy collecting objects related to their journeys, and they also have a certain fondness for vintage board games; there's often a half-finished jigsaw puzzle on a card table for friends to work on while they're catching up. I sensed their nostalgia for the way things were when they were younger, and appreciated my clients both as fun-loving, unaffected people and as Midwesterners connected to a specific time and place. As it used to be said, I knew where they were coming from.

This couple also had an attraction to the lifestyle on Harbour Island, where Thurston Howell III meets Tina Louise, and had decided to get a home of their own in the Bahamas—their first in the tropics. They'd purchased plans for a spec house in a new community, on one of the northernmost Bahamian islands, with sand like pink sugar and a great expanse of impossibly turquoise sea. My clients wanted something in the Caribbean Plantation mode, the kind of style for which the English set designer Oliver Messel, who also created houses, became famous on Mustique.

The directive was to make this a family place, warm, pretty, and easy to live in, a magnet for their five grown children as well as a place to kick back and relax. In communities such as this, where people often rent out their houses when not in residence, interior design can tend toward the impersonal. That was precisely the opposite of what my clients were after; they wanted a home, not a hotel.

Though the house had to remain in the vernacular of the community, I undertook numerous changes to the exterior architecture, making it less generic and more attractive: recladding the façades—with coral on the first floor, clapboard above—and adding Chinese Chippendale railings (my homage to Messel) to the second-floor porches. We also included gas lighting elements, and selected the paint colors and the shutters, which are

PREVIOUS PAGES: A graphic stripe motif—in the carpet, curtains, and paneled poplar walls—prevails in the living room, conveying the flavor of Rat Pack swank. LEFT AND OPPOSITE: I enlivened the front and rear façades with applications of coral stone on the first floor and turquoise clapboard on the second, along with a Chinese Chippendale porch rail panel that pays homage to Oliver Messel's designs on Mustique. The generous forecourt and large pool maximize privacy and spaciousness on the narrow lot with its close-at-hand neighbors.

functional as well as decorative. The lot itself is quite snug, but I was able to create a welcoming forecourt, enclosed by plaster walls and a wooden gate, and an expansive backyard pool that's a conch-shell's throw away from the ocean, so that the grounds feel gracious while also private and self-contained.

Within, I reworked the plan, changing one of the five existing bedrooms into a swank media room, and adding a powder room beneath the stair that's accessed via a secret swinging bookcase, to make it fun. The most significant design gesture involved recladding much of the interior with wood, specifically rough-cut poplar. Most of the houses I saw on the island had Sheetrock walls. Conversely, I wanted this house to possess a certain texture and rusticity, and though poplar is typically painted, it remains quite labile in its unfinished state, which produces an appropriately primitive look. At the same time, we did conceive of the house as being shipshape, so the moldings are all finished with a high gloss, and we limed the poplar ceilings (to make them appear as if bleached by years of salt water). The floors are coral stone, which has a wonderfully natural texture and feels, when you walk in barefoot, almost like an extension of the beach.

The presiding decorative style I would characterize as the Rat Pack Goes to Harbour Island. The house's main floor has the look of a refined beach shack, with low-slung lounge-style seating, a mixture of retro

OPPOSITE: The entry hall features a vintage rattan console table. Seashell-themed decoupage lamps flank a decoupage mirror that reflects a hand-painted mural map of the Abaco Islands. ABOVE: The game table and chairs in the living room create a quiet corner in which to play Parcheesi or chess, or put together a puzzle.

The sweep of the rattan console behind the living room sofa at once complements and contrasts with the lively unpainted wood wall. The predominance of turquoise, here and elsewhere, draws on the magnificent color of the Sea of Abaco, which is visible just outside the window. The turtle above the chairs—hand-carved by a Connecticut artisan—is a reminder not to take beach life too seriously (especially as turtles this size and larger await beyond the back door).

LEFT: A bowl of colorful glass balls (reminiscent of Japanese net floats) rests on the living room's hammered zinc coffee table. OPPOSITE: The dining area sits at the center of the forty-foot-long great room, and is anchored by the table, which recalls a giant ship's winch, adding to the nautical flavor. The spherical, rope-wrapped pendant fixtures, which pair with chairs of woven hemp, guarantee that every day marks a celebration.

and modern pieces, and playful components like the carved wooden turtle hanging from the living room ceiling. The selection of vintage bamboo and rattan furniture captures the essence of what we wanted the design to convey. Dining chairs covered in woven hemp, a hand-hammered galvanized zinc coffee table, mirrored side tables, and a rope chandelier add texture and reflectivity. Fabrics are practical and don't require a lot of care—they invite visitors to flop down and be comfortable, yet there's still a measure of elegance in the well-proportioned furniture and crisply tailored curtains.

If there is one room that seems especially to capture the Midwest-meets-Caribbean spirit, it is the media room, which also serves as the library and, not incidentally, the bar. In contrast to the rest of the house, it is dark—we stained the poplar a rich chocolate, and the bamboo seating, colorful curtains, and textured rug have almost a traditional formality, like a late-nineteenth-century screened porch in a tropical style. The bar sets a different tone: it's a vintage freestanding unit of the sort you would have found in an American basement rec room circa 1962, and we paired it with swiveling stools, a little refrigerator, and a glassware cabinet, so that at five o'clock you're ready for action. The space is finished off with personal elements: books, memorabilia, and family photos. It isn't a big room. But there is everything the family needs to move both forward and backward in time and, above all, to live in the moment.

The bright, open kitchen, with its sea-glass backsplash, serves as a deliberately cheerful contrast to the cozy living area at the room's opposite end.

OPPOSITE AND ABOVE: Distinctly different from the rest of the house, the media room/
bar features rich dark walls and ceiling, balanced by the light-colored hemp and
chenille rug and inviting upholstery, lively curtains, and glossy white crown molding.
A shell lamp and various sea creatures tie the room to the beach and sea beyond.

PREVIOUS PAGES, ABOVE, AND OPPOSITE: Each of the bedroom suites enjoys its own distinctive element: a key lime cannonball bed with elaborately turned spindles or nautically coral-striped curtains, a wall-mounted construction of boat hulls and lures or delightful fish-patterned wallpaper, nail heads forming a fish-scale motif on matching headboards or an "around the world" quilt adding zesty color. The prevailing spirit is that of a beach shack made mature and muscular by a consistency of architectural and decorative elements.

GULF COAST GRANDEUR

When people ask what Naples, on Florida's Gulf Coast, is like, it might be said that it's Palm Beach for Midwesterners. You can see it in the luxury emporia, which address the tastes of a different sort of clientele—Maus & Hoffman and Gattle's, rather than Ralph Lauren or Frette. Whereas Palm Beach is typically tongue-in-cheek, Naples goes a gentler, which is to say more restrained, route. Even the weather seems somehow more like that of the Plains States—softer in character.

When my clients first invited me to have a look, this six-bedroom house struck me as Midwest Tropical. On the plus side, it enjoyed a lovely setting, right on the water and with a harbor view. The place had a kind of Palladian flavor, with the major public rooms connected via a long enfilade of archways. The ceilings on the main floor were eleven feet high, soaring above tall arched windows that filled the rooms with light. On the minus side, though it was meant to be rather grand, the effect proved to be skin-deep; as a high-end spec house, it wasn't as well built or thoughtfully detailed as it might have been.

My fashion-forward client requested that we invest the house with a greater degree of restraint without subtracting its innate elegance—that we make it more reflective of her personal style. I needed to do so, moreover, largely using furniture from a house I'd created for her on the East End of Long Island in the 1980s, beautiful pieces that nonetheless had gotten out of sync with the times.

It is always important for me to get the architectural shell correct. Accordingly, I replaced much of the interior detail, including the crowns, the casings, and windows that leaked, and installed shallow coffered ceilings to add a sense of refinement. As the *parquet de Versailles* in the dining room was dark-stained and overchiseled, I sanded and refinished it, so that the effect felt authentic and less commercial; elsewhere we installed stone floors, which imparted a cool gravitas. The house had many doors, and I persuaded my client to lacquer them a charcoal gray, which helped make the architecture, with its great expanses of Sheetrock, feel less massive. Speaking of color: Decoratively, Naples can suffer from a plague of sherbets. Instead, we painted the rooms in related shades of chocolate, gray, deep blue, and charcoal—very rich, but subdued, calm, and cohesive.

PREVIOUS PAGES: An enfilade of archways, which I strengthened with high-gloss casings, creates a stately cadence on the water-facing side of this Naples residence. Calm shades of dove gray and charcoal brown soothe the mood and layer the spaces. RIGHT: In the dining room, the *parquet de Versailles* floor was sanded, restained, and waxed to make it feel authentic, and the Italian chairs were slipcovered in a heavy embroidered linen that conceals their formal lines. My studio designed the accompanying marquetry table inlaid with exotic woods. The framed jellyfish prints came from a book I gave my client as a Christmas present.

OPPOSITE: The living room's magnificent carved French marriage armoire complements the 1910 bronze torchères and a Moroccan marble chandelier. A 1980s Plexiglas coffee table floats like an ice block in the living room's monochrome sea. Beyond, the study's curtains look as though they were made from a (very tall) Italian sailor's uniform.
ABOVE: Inspired by a stormy ocean day while I was surveying the house, the Venetian blue wall color is a glamorous, atmospheric backdrop for the modern Murano chandelier.

Bringing down the scale of the family room, and making it cozy, proved a major challenge. I sectioned the space with an application of nonstructural ceiling beams infilled with beadboard, and used tailored wool tattersall curtains to soften the architecture's grandiosity; the textured carpet is hand-loomed and sturdy. The coffee table is large enough to eat off of—and everyone does—and showcases a selection of art books; woven jute lounge chairs impart a Caribbean flavor. As for my heroically scaled, custom-designed chenille sectional sofa, it's big enough to hold three hounds, and at least twice as many humans.

194

Roughly three-quarters of the furnishings on the main floor come from my client's previous residence, and it was interesting to see how effectively—when I used my upholstery-design skills to restyle the sofas and slipper chairs—the 1980s profiles could be contemporized. Certain pieces, like the torchères that had been taken from a Christian Science temple in New York, were already classics; others, notably a high-style acrylic coffee table and a handsome set of McGuire dining chairs, emerged from the chrysalis of decorative uncertainty transformed, happily, into "vintage."

It can be tricky to design rooms of this scale: on the one hand, you can't install overly diminutive pieces; on the other, you have to avoid the trap of assuming that just because the spaces are voluminous, what you put in them has to be, too. For example, there had been a gargantuan chandelier in the double-height entry hall that certainly displaced a lot of air but would have made Liberace blush; we replaced it with a more discreet object of my own design, which combined a reflective gazing ball with turned oak, iron scrollwork, and rock crystal, and suggested the restraint of a classic Georgian manor house.

In some cases, I chose to create architecture with furniture, as in the palatial family room, which I zoned into manageability with a chenille-upholstered (and dog-friendly) U-shaped sectional sofa, the epic scale of which is rivaled only by its comfort. Elsewhere, I dealt with an abundance of square footage by embracing it. The master suite exemplifies this: its three areas—with a four-poster bed of my design, a skirted table flanked by armchairs, and a romantic double-sided "tête-à-chaise" (also from my collection) before the fireplace—correspond to the three sets of French windows with their arched fanlights. The bath, with a soaking tub overlooking the water, is the personification of glamour.

To a greater degree than many of my projects, the design of this house proceeded from the need to respond to a series of challenges; as such, it demonstrates the truth of Le Corbusier's indelible maxim that a successful plan is always based on a problem that has been well stated. By forthrightly contending with the structure's architectural limitations and daunting size, and making a thoughtful edit of the existing furniture portfolio, we were able to sculpt the acres of drywall into classic forms, and create a decorative scheme that is elegant, relaxed, and fashion-forward—my client, that most stylish of women, wears the house well.

Classic woven-leather captain's chairs circle a formidable lion-head-and-paw table base carved in linden wood, echoing the colors of the chairs and the English cupboard. A twisted wrought-iron chandelier of my design sits lightly above.

PREVIOUS PAGES, OPPOSITE, AND ABOVE: The master suite was large enough to zone into three distinct areas, and required custom furnishings to fit it—notably the room-within-a-room bed, the accompanying night tables, and the chaise before the fireplace. The custom wool carpet appears crocheted in gray pinstripe, which is echoed in the crewelwork curtains. Dashes of raspberry add a light zest to the soothing pearl-gray mix.

ABOVE AND OPPOSITE: Few things speak more eloquently of luxury than a grand-scaled, well-furnished bath. This one, off the master bedroom, includes a large upholstered ottoman and Neptune chair, and a soaking tub with an incomparable water view, as well as a his-and-hers washstand, a vintage mirror, and multiple lighting sources.

A SUNLIT ROMANCE

ncredibly enough, my clients purchased this California beach bungalow by mistake. The husband was on the phone with a neighbor, discussing the sale of the latter's home, and the wife, overhearing one side of the conversation, took a piece of paper and wrote "Buy It Now!"—in the mistaken belief that it was the house directly *behind* them (which would have afforded the couple more yard space). Somewhat puzzled, but not wanting to disappoint his beloved, the gentleman did as asked—at which point they found themselves in possession of a tiny Cape Cod cottage that was at once near to collapse and subject to strict preservation rules on the exterior. It was an expensive error, but the gentleman was a man of his word; deciding that with a little love, the place would make a fine guesthouse—and aware of the work I had done on my own Shingle-style home in East Hampton—the pair turned to me.

It did not take long for other aspirations to emerge. Though the husband's family has been an influential California presence for many generations, they came originally from Sweden, and he possessed the best of that nation's character: he was modest despite his accomplishments, gentlemanly to a fault, and given to a certain formal reserve. His wife, by contrast, had grown up in Warsaw, and possessed exceptionally sophisticated northern European tastes, which included a love of eighteenth-century furnishings. Though the cottage was meant for guests, the couple began to see it as more formal in design and character and an opportunity to combine their aesthetic heritages.

First, the place had to be entirely reconstructed, which afforded me the opportunity to change the plan, by enlarging the master suite and public rooms and making them freely intercommunicative. To create the flavor of a Scandinavian summer cottage, I introduced wood paneling and a high wainscot, and installed five-panel doors of the sort one might find in a cabin. Because the house was so diminutive, I chose to limit the color palette: We lacquered the entire interior Swiss Coffee, a warm and creamy white, and all of the white oak floors were bleached and stained a shade of gray. Otherwise, a brilliant egg-yolk-yellow hue predominates—I wouldn't use it in Sweden, but the color exudes warmth (even in Southern California's famous "June gloom" season), and serves as a lively background for the furnishings. These are elegant, refined, and, in places, extravagant: a small

Biedermeier breakfast table, a French nineteenth-century daybed in the Louis XVI style, Gustavian neoclassical chairs. Combined with the simple handwoven rugs, embroidered textiles, and fabric-covered walls, they produce an outcome at once elaborate and comfortable, singular and personal.

The cottage played host to precisely one guest—a great Russian maestro. After that, it will not surprise you to learn, the pair began using it as a setting in which to entertain. Then, after spending a few nights in the cottage, and experiencing its charm and intimacy, they decided to renovate their main house and moved into the cottage for a two-year campout. Polish sophistication, Swedish simplicity, and the optimism of California—unlikely perhaps, but a happy, and very apt, combination for a couple that always seemed deeply, happily in love.

PREVIOUS PAGES: In the foyer, glossy beadboard wainscoting (and a playful ceiling); well-apportioned casings, crowns, and baseboards; and a custom-designed wall fabric support refined neoclassical Swedish antiques. The walnut Biedermeier center table stands atop a soft woven wool carpet. The delicate lantern adds a graceful touch. ABOVE: This late eighteenth-century Stockholm case clock reveals rare carving and an even rarer royal provenance. OPPOSITE: Crisp linen whites and egg-yolk yellows radiate a cheerful warmth. The eighteenth-century Gustavian chair harmonizes with the French neoclassical Deco mirrored coffee table.

ABOVE: The sun-filled home encourages guests to relax without sacrificing the elegance of the tailored furnishings. OPPOSITE: Sitting on top of a hand-planed and lye-bleached ash floor, the Biedermeier burl breakfast table, flanked by Gustavian chairs, offers a view of Newport's harbor.

OPPOSITE: Northern European elements influenced the piercing and decoration of the raw wood shutters and painted railings. A romantic garden of espaliered roses, English boxwood, and jasmine embraces the 1920s wrought-iron furniture. ABOVE: Dressed in a floor-length cloth, the breakfast table is accompanied by well-tailored slipcovered chairs with bootstrap buttoning.

I added the veranda off this sunny hideaway. Exquisite embroidered curtains, water silk–upholstered walls, a French neoclassical daybed, and a silver-thread-stitched panel of rococo flourishes suggest a romantic interlude is in the offing.

URBAN COUTURE

The owner of this New York apartment gave me my first big break, engaging my firm to design a beach house that would have been a dream project for any professional. More significantly, as a muse, she has taught me so much about design. An extremely fashionable woman, she's always dressed beautifully, her jewelry is stunning, yet in all matters, there is an exquisite sense of restraint. This instinct of knowing precisely when to stop extends to the rooms she inhabits, and influenced me powerfully in the 1980s, a time in which, as the saying goes, nothing succeeded like excess.

The building, overlooking Manhattan's storied Gramercy Park, was for decades a no-less-storied residence for women, its single-room accommodations hosting generations of aspiring actresses, journalists, and the like, their triumphs and disappointments witnessed by the matron who guarded the door. Eventually, the ghosts of Golightlys past were exorcized by a starchitect, who converted the place into luxury residences. My client chose a floor-through specifically for its relationship to the park. Just a few stories above the treetops, it has expansive city views yet maintains a close connection to the green, its colorful plantings and elegant, rambling plan.

Unfortunately, despite the abundant square footage and natural light, the architect wasn't able to overcome the inherent limitations of what had been, in reality, a boardinghouse. I always tell apartment-dwelling clients that you can't change the height of the ceiling or the size of the windows; here, the former was low, and the latter were oddly placed. The building also suffered from that chronic New York real estate malady, developer-itis. Though there was a "quality" name attached, the walls were thin Sheetrock over metal studs and the fittings and appliances placeholders for the better ones presumably to come.

My client was adamant about not gutting the space—this was to be an interior design job, expressive of her signature well-edited, tightly tailored glamour. But I knew that if the project were to succeed, I had to find a way to infuse it with architectural strength, a *presence*. Our tasks as client and designer fell along familiar lines. She was strongly involved with the decorative aspects; we went shopping together and developed schemes and ideas that drew on what she envisioned. I was entrusted with making the rooms look well balanced and proportional, and doing whatever architectural reinventions I deemed essential.

PREVIOUS PAGES: Throughout this Gramercy Park apartment, we created simple vignettes, composed of vintage-inspired pieces distinguished by their sculptural forms, to showcase and support my client's superlative art collection. Léger's painting sits powerfully above a modern take on the klismos chair. RIGHT: We mirrored one wall of the living room, and inserted portals of polished sycamore, to at once expand and delineate the space and give it architectural sinew. The low profiles of the furnishings compensate for the height-challenged ceiling. The silk carpet and lithe upholstery reflect my client's strong fashion sense: she has a restrained sense of color but an attraction to shimmer, and appreciates fabrics with depth, structure, and complexity.

I began by strengthening the existing elements, and giving the spaces a certain luxurious definition. In the long, undifferentiated living room, I inserted portals constructed from a lacquered and stained curly sycamore, which divided the space and paradoxically made it feel larger, and I mirrored an entire wall, to give the narrow room light and depth, and to capture the great views. Not every gesture was so dramatic: painting the window mullions a dark color gave the anemic glazing greater drama, and an overlay of chic.

Having elevated the architecture, we added another layer of presence via the finishes and the textiles. The walls and doors were glazed and lacquered, and the floors polished to a high gloss. As my client is involved in the world of fashion, she appreciates textiles with richness and complexity, and this impulse found its way into the upholstery and carpets, which shimmer with shades of silver, lavender, aubergine, and gray; in certain rooms, surfaces were given a strié treatment mixing lavender, silver, and opalescence. We also used curtains architecturally, to make the windows seem taller and wider. The lushness of the rugs and the layers of upholstery render the apartment incredibly quiet despite the city's cacophony—even as the rhythms of the textures, patterns, and reflective components bring it, with subtle vibrancy, to life.

The furnishings—and we didn't want a lot of them—had to meet various criteria. Because the ceilings were

OPPOSITE: The wallpaper's kaleidoscopic photography of amethyst quartz serves as a prelude to the master bedroom, where I transformed the absence of a view into an asset. FOLLOWING PAGES: Finished in soothing shades of lavender, the master bedroom is a peaceful sanctuary, layered with plush fabrics. The thick, sound-absorptive carpet mixes silver, gray, and aubergine, and there is an opalescence echoed in the reflective strié finish on the walls. The outcome is a subdued yet luxurious urbanity—and distinctly feminine.

low, the elements needed to keep a comparably low profile; under the circumstances, normal-sized sofas and chairs would have seemed like barriers. At the same time, we wanted the pieces to be sleek, feminine, and curvaceous (and in fact, women look especially seductive seated on furnishings of this shape and scale). Other components are finished with sumptuous materials—there's a beautiful table made of python skin, silver, and nickel—and some are translucent, such as the poured-resin tables and hand-spun glass lamps. Many of our selections are thin and elongated, with plenty of space around them to draw out their striking silhouettes—lithe, almost dancerlike in their qualities.

Perhaps the most compelling element of all, and in many ways the design scheme's raison d'être, is my client's blue-chip art collection, which includes works by Léger, Miró, Picasso, and Degas, to name but a few. Through careful placement and picture lighting, and by "framing" each canvas with curtains or a selection of elegant standing lamps, we were able to make these extraordinary artworks the stars of the show.

The outcome is what I'd call a "real New York apartment"—urbane and edited, at once cheerful and livable, seeming to float on a cloud even though (or perhaps in part because) it's not up all that high; it has the textured, silvery character of a vintage photo by Norman Parkinson or Irving Penn. Most of all, I am proud that in every particular, this Gramercy Park residence seems a reflection of my client's personality—perfectly suited to her special nature.

PREVIOUS PAGES, LEFT: We turned the idea of a traditional foyer on its ear with a very contemporary checkerboard floor of gray and beige limestone. The iron and stone console picks up the lines of the Braque sketch. PREVIOUS PAGES, RIGHT: My client wanted an inviting paneled library. This wallpaper achieved a similar effect in a light-spirited manner. The Cubist sconce echoes the wallpaper's geometric veneers. RIGHT: In the office, the Lucite desk and molten glass lamp continue the theme of transparency. The patterned circles on the wall are actually microscopic cellular images fabricated in laser-cut ebony veneers. FOLLOWING PAGES: The breakfast area in the kitchen, enlivened with boldly colored clay artworks and witty fabrics, continues the design's commitment to reflective strong silhouettes, subdued stylishness, and a minimum of furnishings.

EAST HAMPTON ELEGANCE

As a kid from Kansas City, I always wanted to live at the beach—"Hey, it's only twenty-three hours to the ocean," we used to say—and after establishing myself in New York, I yearned for a place on the water, one where I could have a real garden. In 1999, my husband, Paul, found a long, narrow property on a promontory overlooking Gardiners Bay, on Long Island's South Fork. Incredibly, it was virgin land, overgrown with invasive plants and poison ivy—"a mound of dirt," my good friend Susan called it—but it was just what I'd always wanted.

After going over budget on the lot, we couldn't afford an architect. But having been a designer, at that point, for nearly a decade and a half, I felt confident that I could create the house of our dreams.

I envisioned something in the New England vernacular—a foursquare Greek Revival with Federal details, one that resembled the older classical residences I'd studied and admired in the region—and after doing my usual overabundance of research, I began drawing the house on the weekends, gradually transferring the concept in my head onto drafting vellum. I produced a symmetrical design, owing in part to my love of balance and proportion, but also because, as a first-timer, it was going to be easier for me to pull off. Every aspect of the process intrigued me—even familiarizing myself with the labyrinthine building codes and contending with the structural engineering. At times it could be frustrating. But restrictions impose discipline and inspire creativity, and I benefited in both respects.

As important to the house itself was the design of the landscape, which I zoned into outdoor rooms that related both to one another and to the interior of the residence. The first "beat" of the arrival experience—the motor court—evolved from two directions: I didn't want to reveal the entire property immediately, and I envisioned the garage as a stand-alone pavilion, not attached to the residence suburbia-style. Accordingly, when you arrive in the motor court, which serves as a car park, you encounter an elegant carriage house (also for cars) and a hillock on which I placed a belvedere garden folly. Coming around the carriage house, you open the gate to find yourself on a gravel path directly on axis with a long reflecting pool and, beyond it, the initial reveal of the house.

PREVIOUS PAGES: I designed our home on a bluff overlooking Gardiners Bay, combining Federal, Greek Revival, and Shingle style elements. Styled as a reflecting pool, the swimming pool contributes to the arrival experience. RIGHT: Rich yellow walls, stenciled in a seventeenth-century French pattern, are glazed with seven layers of shellac, enveloping the room in warmth. The classic columns, doors, and casings are painted in gloss to capture the shimmer of the sea. Deeply inviting upholstery, a commodious coffee table, side tables for books, and slipcovered ottomans form a floor plan that invites conviviality. A Swedish wall clock on the mirror hovers over an eighteenth-century English mantel faced with Delft tiles picturing sailing vessels. The proportions of the room—based on the golden rectangle—feel just right.

PERIOD FINISHES AND EFFECTS   JUDITH AND MARTIN MILLER

OXFORD COLLEGE GARDENS   Tim Richardson   LL

HISTORIC HOUSES OF PARIS
RESIDENCES OF THE AMBASSADORS   Flammarion

OPPOSITE: The shuttered partial wall on which a dazzling Italian starburst mirror reflects the sea lightly separates the living room from the entry. The column screen is replicated on the exterior to create indoor/outdoor continuity. RIGHT: A thoughtfully detailed Swedish bergère sits next to the majolica pedestal that inspired the living room's golden wall color.

The pool—which does indeed reflect the structure—imparts a soothing sense of grandeur to the second "beat." As with so many of the project's components, its location represented a mix of necessity and desire: on the one hand, there wasn't room for it on either side of the house—and on the other, I wanted to avoid the character of a suburban splash box, with lounge chairs and fringed umbrellas over drinks tables. Placing the pool where I did gives the garden a sense of surprise and delight, creating the perfect prelude to the culminating experience of the residence.

As for the house's program, I did what I do with my clients: I interviewed myself and Paul, asking what we desired and how we wanted to live. What I discovered was that we appreciated the pleasures of an open plan on the main floor but didn't want to sacrifice the discretion of individual rooms. I knew as well that a fireplace (with space for seating around it) remained a priority, as did having water views from every window of every room. I continued to wrestle with architectural challenges, most notably the staircase: where to put it and how to design it. Originally I had a straight run up to the second floor, until I realized that with an eleven-foot ceiling height downstairs, I'd need paramedics to get me past the midpoint. So I discovered a way to turn the stair around several landings.

ABOVE: A carved beechwood table creates a muscular silhouette before the generously scaled window. My favorite hydrangea-filled blue-and-white jardinières flank this English antique, while large custom pedestals are guarded by a pair of heroically scaled urns. OPPOSITE: The layering of patterns invites the guest to view the sea beyond.

OPPOSITE: For years I wanted to line my portals with Delft tiles—here featuring harbor scenes with windmills—after being mesmerized by Charles de Beistegui's similarly lined library window wells. FOLLOWING PAGES: The dining room's Wedgwood blue walls unite the room with Gardiners Bay, and the silver reflects the sparkling view. It is a seaside beach house, and meant to be comfortable and relaxed. This is not incompatible with a certain formal elegance, and a high level of finish and detail—evident in the dining room's Scandinavian sideboard, high-gloss stenciled floor, and paneled cathedral ceiling. Here, sentimental to a fault, I placed my grandmother's dining table and my parents' chairs.

I drew, and redrew, the home's layout, starting with an idealized plan, then fiddling with the size and proportions of each component—mediating between measurements and intuition. The doorways were tweaked to create enfilades that facilitate light, views, cross-ventilation, and easy communication between rooms. I crafted furniture plans, making sure to have the right number of seating areas in the living room, enough chairs at the dining table, and sufficient space in the guest room for two night tables, a comfortable chair, and a chest of drawers. Ultimately, all of the rethinking paid off: I came up with a perfectly proportioned living room, following the principles of the golden rectangle, that also served the holy trinity of TV, fireplace, and views. At the four corners, I placed the kitchen, dining room, guest room, and library—spaces that both function well and feel right. And there are multiple ways into and out of the house, making the interior and exterior connections entirely, satisfyingly seamless.

The project also served as a laboratory of sorts, enabling me to put into practice many of the principles I'd developed as a designer, to check them against my own feelings and responses as a homeowner. What I discovered was that a sense of well-being was the first, most essential principle, and all the others developed from and supported it. Fluidity, for example: I wanted to be drawn into and through each space at

the right tempo, and to feel welcome and comfortable as I did so. Each room—especially spaces that we typically think of as being more ceremonial, like the formal living room—needed at least one strongly defined function, and ideally more than one. Light, of course, is an essential component of well-being, and I made sure the house was filled with it. As I worked on the design, what came strongly to the fore was the significance of detail: the trim on the curtains, the welting of the sofa, even the kinds of bulbs in the chandelier—all the elements that enhance and intensify experience and make a room feel complete. And, not least, proportion: the harmonious composition of the architecture, as well as its relationship to the furniture and, naturally, the human scale. All of these principles had come into play, to a greater or lesser degree, on my previous projects. But adjusting them to my own sense of personal satisfaction increased my understanding of their value, and gave them even greater resonance.

We've now been in the house for over fifteen years, and I appreciate it more with each passing season. Paul and I entertain almost every weekend, and whether it's a benefit for three hundred or dinner for six, the place feels just right; everyone says it's "a big little house." The project taught me a lot: to respect what my clients go through; why architects deserve every penny they earn; that if you're willing to invest time and creativity, you can resolve almost any design challenge. Without question, my home made me the designer that I am today.

Our place taught me something else as well, which I will readily convey to anyone who will listen. Simply this: Your nest isn't a commodity, or a real estate venture. It's home—and if that's what drives all your decisions, really, you can't go wrong.

OPPOSITE: The coffee-colored entry foyer, between my grandfather's chairs, opens into the front hallway, and faces the shuttered wall separating the arrival experience from the living room. Buffed limestone floors and the row of bronze lanterns draw your eye toward the guest room beyond. FOLLOWING PAGES: A paneled cathedral ceiling in the master suite is graphically emphasized by a dark khaki gloss, and houndstooth, glen plaid, and checked patterns. Charcoal colors complement the honeyed tiger maple of the secretary and the four-poster bed.

ABOVE: The guest bath is fitted with twin sinks and an unusual Dutch pine commode for maximum graciousness. OPPOSITE: In the guest room, an enticing mélange of camel, café au lait, crème, and willow prevails.

OPPOSITE: The Federal entry portico is surrounded by lush plantings. My garden and gardening are essential to my life. ABOVE: The raised belvedere offers a view of the water. FOLLOWING PAGES: I designed the façade of the pool house to be in sympathy with the architecture of the main house—on this side; the other façade, facing the motor court, resembles a Shingle-style carriage house. A pebble and stone pathway toward the bluff draws you from the house to a table overlooking the bay, one of our favorite dining spots.

ACKNOWLEDGMENTS

Though *The Art of Elegance* is written in the first person, in almost every instance, the pronoun "I" could have been replaced by "we." The great reward—and pleasure—of our profession lies in its inherent nature of collaboration. I have never traveled this journey alone, but always with the guidance, encouragement, dedication, and friendship of numerous talented people.

In particular, the remarkably gifted designers, draftspeople, and assistants on our team, who have uniformly shouldered and shared every task in the design process with integrity, perseverance, and creativity. It has been a privilege—and enormous fun—to work alongside Chris Welsh, Kate Reid, Jeffrey Kilmer, Scott Hickman, Wendy Monette, Mercedes Ganes, Tara Kates, Alissa Deane, and Melissa Powell.

We have been blessed to be able to offer our clients the highest-achieving technical wizardry of so many gifted workrooms and artisans, who at the same time have taught me so much. In particular, through long association and friendship, I would like to thank decorative artist Judy Mulligan, curtain tailor Gary Ruesch, and upholsterer Gatebirth (Joe) Joseph.

I have the deepest respect for architects, and have been fortunate to have worked with some great ones, including Mark Critchfield, Stephen Wang, Alan Wanzenberg, Raul Lastra, and my most frequent collaborator, Stephen Morgan. And I am no less grateful for the overworked, overstressed, and often under-appreciated contractors, who have meticulously and patiently materialized our dreams: Steve MacMillan, John Petrocelli, BCB Homes, Carl Akin, Magnus Bjorklund, Leslie Page, Jan Robinson, and Chouteau Building Group. Finally, a passion for gardening has led me to hold in high esteem the landscape designers with whom I have been very lucky to work: Garr Campbell, Jack deLashmet, Craig Socia, and Nord Eriksson.

In realizing this book, I wish to thank Aliza Fogelson and Kathleen Jayes for their insightful contributions, and Charles Miers for the honor of publishing with Rizzoli. My deepest gratitude goes to wordsmith Marc Kristal for insisting on "my indelible footprint" and sculpting my voice in a way I could not; book designers Doug Turshen and Steve Turner for their elegant graphic ingenuity; the photographers, whose brilliant artistry has so beautifully captured our work; and most of all Jill Cohen for her doctoral guidance and her unrelenting belief in my work. Thanks are also due to the unflappable problem-solving of Melissa Powell, whose dedication to getting this book right is the glue that has bound the disparate parts together; to Susan Kelly, whose opinions and friendship have been an inspiration throughout this whole process; and to Deborah Devine, on whose calming influence, insight, and care we all depend.

My gratitude extends as well to all the talented, encouraging editors and photographers at these magazines for supporting our work: *Architectural Digest*, *Veranda*, *House Beautiful*, *House & Garden*, *Luxe*, *The New York Times*, *Traditional Home*, *Coastal Living*, *Hamptons Cottages & Gardens*, *New York Spaces*, and in particular, the *Southampton Press*, which has given me almost a decade of bylines to voice my impressions and experiences.

Albert Schweitzer so generously said, "Each of us has cause to think with deep gratitude of those who have lighted the flame within us." Thank you to the mentors and teachers who have lighted that flame within me: Matt Kahn, William Eddelman, Lucylee Chiles, Mel Bishop, Nancy Clausen, Gary Crain, Steve Mittman, Grandie, and Uncle Jack.

To my parents who encouraged me to follow my passion; to my brother Tom, who followed his; and to my brother Ridge, who not only followed his passion, but believed in us all. To Susan, who tenaciously believed that this book could happen and encouraged me unconditionally, and to Paul, who makes me laugh every day.

And finally, to all the generous homeowners who are not only our friends and muses, but who have also trusted us with their dreams, their visions, and the opportunity to co-create such beauty, such elegance. They have all allowed us to enter their worlds and leave behind an imprint of comfort and home.

CREDITS

Mary Ellen Bartley: 233

Pieter Estersohn: 89, 98

Tria Giovan Photography: 255

Max Kim-Bee: 7 (top row right), 75, 76-77, 79, 80-81, 82-83, 84-85, 86-87, 123, 124-125, 126, 127, 128-129, 130, 131, 132-133, 134, 135, 136-137, 250, 252, 253, 256-257

Francesco Lagnese: 4-5, 15, 16-17, 18-19, 20-21, 22, 23, 24-25, 26, 27, 28, 30-31, 169, 170-171, 172, 173, 174, 175, 176-177, 178, 179, 180-181, 182, 183, 184, 185, 186, 187, 194-195, 197, 201, 216, 218-219, 220, 221, 222, 223, 224-225, 226, 227, 228-229, 230, 231

David Duncan Livingston: 138, 140, 141, 142-143, 144, 145, 146-147, 148, 149, 151, 152-153, 154-155, 156-157, 158, 159

Keith Scott Morton: 6 (top row left)

Alise O'Brien: 161, 162-163, 164-165, 166

Geno Perches: 2-3, 6 (middle row left), 90-91, 92, 93, 94, 95, 97, 99

Melissa Powell: 251

Lisa Romerein: 11, 54, 56, 57, 58, 59, 60, 61, 62-63, 64-65, 66-67, 68, 69, 70, 71, 72-73, 204, 206, 207, 208, 209, 210, 211, 212, 213, 214-215

Werner Straube Photography: 10, 167, 189, 190-191, 192, 193, 198-199, 200, 202, 203

Luke White: 1, 7 (top row left), 8, 13, 33, 34, 35, 36-37, 39, 40, 41, 42, 43, 44, 45, 46-47, 48, 49, 50-51, 52, 53, 101, 102, 103, 104-105, 107, 108, 109, 110-111, 112-113, 114-115, 116, 117, 118, 119, 120, 121, 234-235, 236, 237, 238, 239, 240, 241, 242, 243, 245, 246-247, 248, 249

Endpapers: Ted Tyler for TylerGraphic

First published in the United States of America in 2017
by Rizzoli International Publications, Inc.
300 Park Avenue South
New York, NY 10010
www.rizzoliusa.com

© 2017 by Marshall Watson

Designed by Doug Turshen and Steve Turner

2018 2019 2020 / 10 9 8 7 6 5 4 3

Distributed in the U.S. trade by Random House, New York

Printed in China

ISBN-13: 978-0-8478-5871-2

Library of Congress Catalog Control Number: 2016950646